www.cyconsocialmedia.com

www.cyconsocialmedia.com

Small Business MarketingBlueprint

Increase Profits by 20% in 100 Days or Less

by
Duke Morris

www.cyconsocialmedia.com

© 2012 by Duke Morris

Published by CyCon Consulting, LLC

ISBN-13: 978-1480245839

ISBN-10: 1480245836

All Rights Reserved. No part of this publication may be reproduced in any form or by any means, including scanning, photocopying, or otherwise without prior written permission of the copyright holder.

First Printing, 2012

Printed in the United States of America

Income Disclaimer

This document contains business strategies, marketing methods and other business advice that, regardless of my own results and experience, may not produce the same results (or any results) for you. I make absolutely no guarantee, expressed or implied, that by following the advice below you will make any money or improve current profits, as there are several factors and variables that come into play regarding any given business.

Primarily, results will depend on the nature of the product or business model, the conditions of the marketplace, the experience of the individual, and situations and elements that are beyond your control.

As with any business endeavor, you assume all risk related to investment and money based on your own discretion and at your own potential expense.

Liability Disclaimer

By reading this document, you assume all risks associated with using the advice given below, with a full understanding that you, solely, are responsible for anything that may occur as a result of putting this information into action in any way, and regardless of your interpretation of the advice.

You further agree that our company cannot be held responsible in any way for the success or failure of your business as a result of the information presented below. It is your responsibility to conduct your own due diligence regarding the safe and successful operation of your business if you intend to apply any of our information in any way to your business operations.

Terms of Use

You are given a non-transferable, "personal use" license to this product. You cannot distribute it or share it with other individuals.

Also, there are no resale rights or private label rights granted when purchasing this document. In other words, it's for your own personal use only.

Contents

Introduction   11

Are You Leaving Money on the Table? 13
Mistake #1: Going After New Customers   14

Mistake #2: Not Effectively Using Cross-sells, Up-sells or "Package" Selling   17

Mistake #3: Not Understanding the Lifetime Value of a Customer   21

Center of Influence Marketing   25

How to Find Customers for Life   29
The Forgotten "Rule" Of An Obscure Italian Economist   30

Where To Start   31

Referral Marketing Goldmine   35
The power of "Word of Mouth"   35

The Referral System, Step by Step   37

Tear Down Customer Resistance 45
The Selling Power of Testimonials   48

How to Become an Avid Testimonial Collector   49

How to Use Testimonials for Maximum Effect   51

The Anatomy of a Good Testimonial   53

Right Way to Place Yellow Page Ads   55
The Most Important Part of Your Ad   56

Have an Offer And a "Call To Action"   59

5 Proven Internet Strategies to Explode Your Local Sales   61

1 Video Marketing   61

#2 Lead-Capture and Follow-up Campaigns   62

3 Local Search Visibility   63

4 Social Media Marketing   64

5 Blog Marketing   65

About the Author   67

Other books published by Duke Morris: 68

Resources   70

www.cyconsocialmedia.com

www.cyconsocialmedia.com

Small Business Marketing Blueprint

Increase Profits by 20% in 100 Days or Less

Introduction

Do you know what is the most profitable skill necessary for running a small business?

It's not keeping the shelves fully stocked. It's not managing and training employees. It's not even having a good product or service.

No. The most important skill is marketing your business. Why? Well, the only time you can bring money into your business is if you sell something. You can't stock your shelves unless you have money to buy the stuff to put on those shelves.

That's where marketing comes in. It's how you communicate to the public that you have a good product, that you offer a good consumer experience and that they should buy stuff from you, rather than one of your competitors.

Marketing is also the most misunderstood skill today. Poor Marketing is very likely why 65% of new businesses close their doors after 2 years, and over 85% of businesses don't make it 8 years before going under.

Most of your competition simply does not understand how to do marketing properly… in order to bring in amazing results in little to no time. So just knowing a few simple things will put you at a great marketing advantage.

"In the land of the blind, the person with one eye is KING"!

You are about to learn the 7 most powerful – and profitable – marketing strategies that you can start using today, to become the "king" in your own local marketplace, and all within 3 months time or less.

You have right now, in your hands, information that could change your business and life forever. Use it and profit from it.

All the best!

www.cyconsocialmedia.com

Are You Leaving Money on the Table?

Do you know what the 3 Deadly Mistakes are that almost all small businesses are making? And if you don't, well you are not alone. Most entrepreneurs simply have never considered the fact that by making these 3 small tweaks to their current business, they could possibly increase sales by up to 20% within the next 100 days. And it's absolutely true.

I know that some of these ideas may shock you… And in fact I hope they do. Why? Because my job is to help you take a fresh look at your own business, and evaluate the areas that can be improved right now in order to create more sales and improve your bottom line, immediately.

Mistake #1: Going After New Customers

Yes, you read that right. New customers are the most expensive people in the world to find, attract into your place of business, and then convert into accounts receivable.

To help you understand this, let me demonstrate to you this powerful fact.

Simply, there are only 3 ways to increase your profits.

The first way is to increase number of your customers. If Joe has a lemonade stand and sells 100 cups a day to 100 people and makes $0.10 a cup for a total of $10 a day in profit... If Mike figures out a way to get 200 people to buy a cup of lemonade that same day, he's just doubled his profits.

But that's not the only way Joe can double his profit. What if he figures out a way for his customers to purchase two cups of lemonade each? By doing so, he will be able to double his profits with the same number of existing customers.

And what if Joe were to offer something for his customers to purchase that is complimentary to the lemonade... maybe a hot dog? Then, if a certain percentage also buys a hot dog when he sells them lemonade, he can double his sales.

So let's review: here are the only three ways that you will ever be able to to grow your business and increase your profits:

- More customers
- Same customers purchase more stuff
- Same customers making more frequent purchases

Of the three, which is the most profitable? Well, let's look at it like this. Let's say you spend $2,500 a year on a yellow page ad, and it brings you in 100 prospective customers.

You have paid $25 for each person that has come into your store who might purchase from you. That is a static cost. You pay that $25 if they buy nothing from you, or if they buy everything in the store. Doesn't matter.

So what if you could increase the average transaction value for each customer by just $10? What would it cost you? Usually, nothing but a few minutes of creative thinking. You already paid $25 to get them in the store so you might as well maximize their value.

In Joe's case, he "cross-sold" them on a hot dog. It's just a matter of creatively packaging complimentary goods and using the right language to get the highest number of people to say yes to buying something in addition to what they originally came in to the store to purchase.

McDonald's simply asks: "Do you want fries with that?" Extra cost for McDonald's to do that: 2 seconds of training for the employee, and 2 seconds for the employee to say it to each customer.

The result: an overall bump of about $0.08 in profit per customer. And when you have "over 1 billion served", no argue that's a lot of profit!

So here's rule number 1: Spend more of your advertising budget and time on figuring out how to get customers who have purchased from you in the past, or your new prospects, to PURCHASE MORE from you.

Often times the last thing you need is more customers. Whatever problems you currently have in your business, they usually multiply when you bring more customers into the funnel. Instead, figure out how to get MORE from the same number of customers.

Which brings us to Rule Number 2: You must figure out how to get your existing customers to make more frequent purchases from you.

Here's everything required in order to make your marketing work.

- They have to know you exist
- They have to want and be able to afford what you offer
- They have to trust you

You see, new customers first need to hear about you. But that's not enough. They also have to be in the market for what you offer. It's hard to sell ice cream to Eskimos, in spite of some humorous stories.

And finally, they have to trust you enough to exchange their hard-earned dollars for the value you promise to deliver to them in your product or service.

Your current customers, on the other hand, already know you exist, and have already demonstrated that they need at least some of what you offer and at least at one point in their life they trusted you enough to exchange their dollars for the value you promised them.

All else being equal, who do you think is going to be more inclined to say yes to your next offer? A stranger -- or someone who knows you and is likely to be comfortable dealing with you again?

I think the answer is obvious. Before we go into how to get past customers to increase the frequency from which they purchase from you, let's first deal with increasing the average purchasing size from each customer.

Mistake #2: Not Effectively Using Cross-sells, Up-sells or "Package" Selling

We already discussed "cross sells" with "do you want fries with that?" example. So what does this mean for your business? The first thing you need to do is implement your own cross-sells.

Here's a simple way to do that. Look at your 5 to 7 most popular sellers in your business. Each one of them should have a cross-sell. For example in the flooring business, when people buy carpeting, you should also have a special offer for them to buy "spot remover" along with their carpeting.

You can even give them a special "purchase discount" because you don't need as high a margins since you have already PAID (in marketing and advertising) to attract them to come in the door and purchase from you.

So select your five biggest sellers, and find other items that you can offer that complement these main purchases, just like fries compliment a cheeseburger.

Then, just create a quick script to use and to train your employees to use this technique in all situations. It could be something as simple as "Would you be interested in receiving a special 60% purchaser discount on spot remover to complement your flooring purchase today?"

Anything is better than nothing. Based on tests, even a weak attempt at a cross-sell works 6%-20% of the time. The point being is that cross sells have almost no hard cost at all to implement, so why not do it, you may ask yourself.

The second thing is the up-sell. This is where you try to offer them a more expensive or premium version of what they are ready to purchase. Let's return to the flooring example.

There are different pads you can put under your carpet. There is the basic pad, often made of several different materials that are bonded together, thus making it cheaper to sell to clients. Then there is "prime" pad, which is solid, more durable, makes the flooring last longer, but is more expensive.

In this case, when putting together an offer for the customer, you'd want to say something like this "Would you like to invest a little bit more to make this carpet last 6 years longer – and feel more comfortable under your feet?"

Then, you simply explain why buying the upgraded version of the padding is a far better option for them.

Now think about it – if your markup is the same for both types of padding, then you'll make more money if you sell them more expensive carpet pad. Example: let's say you make 50% profit on each pad you sell. If a customer needs 100 square yards of the basic pad, and that sells for $4.50 per square yard, then you just sold $450 of materials, of which $225 is profit to you.

But what if you could bump them up to the premium pad that sells for $7.50 per square yard? Now that's $750 in material sold, of which $375 is profit to you.

That's an increase of $150 for just a few minutes of sales work. Again, all you have to do is come up with a simple script, and a simple way to demonstrate why the little bit of extra cost involved for the customer is worth the investment in terms of what they're going to get for that little extra bit of cost.

So how can you make this work for you? Go back to those 5-7 popular products and simply ask yourself -- "Is there an upgraded and/or premium version of this that I can offer to my customers?"

There always is. And often times, you can make a premium version without hardly any additional hard cost, if you focus on intangibles. Here's an example.

Let's say you own a high-end restaurant. One premium version you can offer to your clients is the "immediate seating" club. For a small fee each year, these customers can guarantee that they get seated as soon as they enter the restaurant.

In this case, you're selling time and convenience, not a product. That may have a lot of value in this day and age.

Or you could even create a special area for preferred customers that has a much more luxurious feel to it, to make them enjoy the atmosphere more. Again, you're selling luxury, not a product, another intangible.

The final sales technique you should consider using is "Packaged Selling". Most people prefer to have someone else make the decision for them, so they don't have any responsibility in the matter.

Let's return to the flooring example. Why not create an "Active Lifestyle Package". This would be for people with young children, maybe pets as well, or for those who have high traffic homes.

For this special package, you choose the carpet, padding, vinyl and tile options, and then sell it as a package, instead of each component on its own. This allows you to already include the premium versions, or the products that have the highest profit margins.

Your customers are more likely to say yes, if you do it right, since it's easier for them to say yes.

Then, the next logical step is to up-sell them to an even more deluxe package. Ha! In this case it could be the "Active and Luxurious Lifestyle Package."

Let's go back to our restaurant example. Let's design the "Romance Package". In this case, the customer would get a limo to pick them up at their door, they get a special table near the fireplace that is more secluded, they get a vase filled with beautiful flowers that they get to take home and keep (including the vase), and they get a special "Lover's Dessert" for the lucky couple to share.

You're no longer in the restaurant business, you're in the romance business and you can charge a lot more for that! Promise.

At the very least, you need to create one "package" that you can offer to a certain portion of your clients. Make it much higher priced and more luxurious than normal so that even if only a handful of customers say yes to it each year, you'll have made a pretty good extra bit of profits without doing hardly any more extra work.

Mistake #3: Not Understanding the Lifetime Value of a Customer

If you knew the potential lifetime value of even an average customer, you'd spend far more time making sure existing customers continued to use your services, and far less time trying to get new customers.

Let me give you an example. Let's say Jill is 45 and spends $100 a week at her preferred grocery store. Lucy doesn't plan on moving any time soon, and has at least 15 more years of good shopping left in her.

So let's see, 15 years is 780 weeks. And at an average of $100 a week, that's $78,000. If you owned that grocery store, don't you think it would be prudent to come up with a strategy to make sure Jill keeps coming back to you and make sure you collect that $78,000?

Now get this. A famous study done some 20 years ago, that was recently just re-tested and re-confirmed, found out what causes people to change and quit going to a store or an existing service provider. Here are the results.

- 9% - Leave because of aggressive competition

OK, so someone else might come along offering them a better deal, or better service. Or perhaps they have a location that's closer than yours. It sucks, but that is part of the game. Nonetheless the instructive and comforting thing to recognize is that you only lose 9% of your customers because of this.

- 9% - Leave because they move

It's hard to get someone to come back to your store if they move halfway across the country. It's just the nature of the beast. Some will move because we are by nature nomadic creatures.

- 14% - Leave because of a complaint or dissatisfaction with your service or product.

Okay, this can be worked on a bit, but one thing I've learned in business is you can't please everyone, nor do you want to. Anyway, it's not that big of a deal, because there is something far, far greater that causes your customers to go somewhere else.

It is greater than all these other factors combined. Here it is:

68% - Leave because of perceived apathy of the service provider.

In other words, they feel you only look at them as a customer to get money from, and that you don't care about them. Notice the word perceived. You might very well care about them, but if you don't show them you care about them in a way that's unique and that isn't something that everyone else does, then there is no reason for them to remain loyal to you.

So if you don't have a specific "customer retention" strategy in place, you're losing 2/3rds of your previous customers. When you consider the potential lifetime value of a customer, that should make you very sick to your stomach.

So what's the remedy? First, you need to increase the amount of communication you have with your past customers. At the very least, follow the "4 a day rule". Every business day, someone in your business should contact at least 4 past customers with a personal follow up, either by email, phone, letter or in person.

You should also consider a newsletter and no, not those fancy, beautiful and "corporate looking" newsletters I'm sure your familiar with. You need to take a much more personal approach.

People don't fall in love with corporations. They fall in love with personalities. The first part of that word is "person". You have to open up to them. Let them know who you are and a little bit about what's going on in your life. You also have to show some character and a bit of humor, and style.

Think of why you're close friends with the friends you're close with. You should try to establish that same bond with your customers. There are several strategies I use to do this, i.e. with a monthly newsletter.

Finally, someone who cares about you looks out for your best interest with no ulterior motive in mind. Again, that's where a newsletter comes in handy. Each month, you can create an article giving them tips on how to better their life, improve the value they can get from your services, and just things that can make them feel better about themselves. And they're getting all this stuff just because they're a customer of yours.

That's one way how you make someone feel special.

At any rate, you need to create some kind of customer retention campaign, and that's often just staying in contact with past customers, once every few months to let them know you're still thinking about them.

www.cyconsocialmedia.com

www.cyconsocialmedia.com

Center of Influence Marketing

Traditional advertising is a complete waste of money. Why? Because traditional or "normal" advertising will get you normal results. You don't become an industry leader or a dominant marketing presence by doing things the "normal" way.

Most small businesses advertise in the Yellow Pages. However, I think you're going to find Yellow Page advertising is going to become weaker and weaker, because more people now use the Internet to find information they need.

Besides, almost all Yellow Page ads look the same. Hmmmm... could it be because they're all designed by the same person? Of course, this means that everybody's ad is by definition "normal".

Newspaper advertising is also falling. But let's look at it – again almost all the ads look the same, more or less. Could it be because they're all designed by the same person? Hmmm... If everything looks normal, everybody gets normal results.

Finally, consider this – you're advertising in the same place as your competitors. That's kind of dumb, isn't it? I'd rather advertise in a vacuum, where I'm the only choice.

You need to think outside the box. I fashion myself as a collector of good ideas. I look for those different ways of advertising that don't get normal results but extraordinary results.

What I'm about to show you is going to give you a far greater return than normal advertising ever will. It will also dramatically enhance the relationship you have with your fellow business owners and finally it'll just make others think you're some sort of genius because of your innovation.

I'm talking about center of influence marketing. Here's the premise – instead of going out hunting down your ideal prospects, what would happen if you already went to where a bunch of them hang out, and just put your sign up in front of them?

You're going to where they already are, instead of picking them up "one by one" in the newspaper, on the television, or in the Yellow Pages.

Okay, so here's what you're going to do – you're going to come up with a bunch of different places where your ideal customers frequent in large numbers. Then you're going to construct an offer that will allow you to siphon those ideal customers off into your own sales funnel. And, it's only going to cost you a small "toll booth" fee to do this, which you will only pay out of a portion of the profits you're generating.

Let' take a second to talk about targeted marketing. Say you and I both owned a pizza place. I would only need one competitive advantage, and I could destroy you and win every single customer. I'd give you all other advantages, because, when totaled, they still wouldn't give you a chance.

Yes, I would give you the best ingredients. I'd give you the best employees. I'd give you the best location. I'd give you the coolest store layout. I'd only ask for one thing.

I'd only ask that all my customers are dying of hunger.

When someone is hungry, they don't care what your store looks like. They don't care if you have good service. They don't care if the food even tastes good. They are just so hungry that they'll practically pay anything and eat anything to quell that hunger.

What targeted marketing does is isolates and focuses your efforts on singling out those who are "hungriest" for whatever you have to offer.

Let me make it real to you. Let's say you're in the retail flooring business. Okay, now people who buy flooring, what else do they tend to need that complements that?

Well, a lot of people who need flooring also need paint. What would happen if you had a majority of the paint stores sending the customers who needed flooring your way?

If I wanted to market to small businesses to offer my marketing consultation services, where would I go? Well, I'd start with the local accountants, because they help a lot of business owners with their taxes.

I would also go to the heads of trade associations that small business owners would be a member of, like the chambers of commerce, for example, and volunteer for free to give a speech where I'd share my expertise on how to get more customers.

I would go to attorneys that help people form corporations, and attorneys who otherwise specialize in helping small businesses.

See what I'm doing here? I'm finding a complementary, non-competitive business entity that already attracts the "hungry" customers that I'm in search of. Instead of having to find those customers myself, I'm leveraging their efforts.

Now, here's how to not make this work. Go up to one of these centers of influence and say, "Hey, why don't you tell your customers to come to me when they need XYZ." This is completely ridiculous.

You have to make it make sense for them to refer others to you before they will, if it makes sense to them. What's an easy way to do this? Why not say, "Hey, I know from time to time you have customers that also need my services. So how do you feel about this? Every time you send someone over my way, and they become my customer, I give you X% of the sale?"

Warning – in some industries, it's illegal to do this. And since I'm not a lawyer, check the laws first to make sure that you can legally do this. I'm just giving you one example here. There are other ways you can reward them.

For example, send customers to them in return. It could be as simple as making a stack of fliers up to put in their business, and they do likewise to distribute at your business. Now it's a "referral revolving door" and more importantly it's a win-win situation.

Here's how you can make it work for you. First, pull out the Yellow Pages. Go through them, and each time you find a category that would be complementary to your business, write it down.

Get 5-10 different complementary "industries", and then pick the top 3 businesses in each of those industries. Now you have a list of 15-30 businesses to approach.

Second, create your irresistible offer for these businesses. If you can give them a cash incentive for a referral, then consider that as your offer. Or come up with something equally enticing that answers their number one question -- "What's in it for me?"

Another thing you can do here is to give a special offer just for their customers. It could be a discount, or something extra they get for free that you would normally charge for. This way, the "What's in it for me?" is that their customers will like them more, because it looks like the owner went to bat and negotiated a special deal just for them.

How many businesses could you do this with? Well, as many as you would like. This can take care of the new customer acquisition end of things, especially when you combine it with referral marketing.

Think about it – you could easily get ten businesses that were complementary to you to promote for you for some sort of attractive incentive.

For some, it might just be that you put up some fliers at the counter, with a special "freebie" just for their customers. For other businesses, it might be a customer exchange. You send customers their way if they send customers your way. For others still, it might work to downright pay them a cut of the sales.

In any case, realize the importance behind this – most of the cost for customer acquisition will only be paid after the customer is acquired. You pay a percentage of the sale – after the sale is made. You get referrals because you refer.

This truly takes the risk out of advertising, because you'll only pay for it if it works. Surely, not a bad deal.

How to Find Customers for Life

Imagine that there was a huge amount of oil buried right outside in your backyard. And we're talking millions of dollars worth.

Would that make you rich? Not if you didn't know about it. You could live your whole life sitting on "liquid gold" and be none the wiser.

However, if I came up to you and told you about it, and showed you beyond a shadow of doubt that there was oil and you drilled for it. Then you'd become filthy rich.

In most small business, there does exist a situation that is similar to the oil well example above. Most small business owners are sitting on a potential fortune and they don't even realize it.

In this chapter I'm going to share with you perhaps the single most effective strategy for mining the "hidden gold" that is likely to exist in your business backyard.

The Forgotten "Rule" Of An Obscure Italian Economist

In 1906 a man by the name of Vilfredo Pareto discovered something unusual about the Italian economy – 80% of the wealth was controlled by 20% of the population.

Was this just an anomaly? Turns out it wasn't. In Britain he found the same thing to be true and found it to be true in pretty much all other economies. But what's interesting is that this unequal distribution exists outside of economies as well. For example, studies have shown in general that:

80% of you traffic accidents are committed by 20% of drivers

80% of crimes are committed by 20% of the population

80% of a company's output comes from 20% of its employees, and most importantly of all...

80% of your profits come from only 20% of your customers!

This is almost always true. So what does that mean for you?

Simple: if you can isolate who those "20 percenters" are, and then come up with a marketing plan that will attract more customers like those "20 percenters" and also create additional products, services and offers for your "20 percenters" then...

You should be able to, very easily, add 20% to your bottom line profits within the next 90 days.

Where To Start

In an ideal situation, you've kept track of your past customer's purchases, so you can access their records. What you want to do is go through and first isolate customers who have spent the most money with you.

Now, that doesn't necessarily mean that they are your most profitable customers. They are just your highest grossing customers. Unfortunately, gross does not always mean more profitable. However, it's a good place to start.

After you find your highest grossing customers, then analyze your profit margin on those customers, to narrow it down even more. To make it easy for you, come up with your 50 "highest grossing customers", and out of those 50, arrange them in order of most profitable, in terms of percentages.

Now take your 20 "Most profitable" customers, and analyze them. What we are looking for are demographics and psychographics.

Demographics are things such as:

- Size of Household
- Annual Income Earned
- Age
- Gender
- Geographical Location
-

Psychographics are:

- What clubs they belong to
- What their hobbies and interests are
- Their Values

- Their Opinions

- Lifestyle & other behavior attributes

In other words, you are trying to isolate their "culture" if you will.

How can this be helpful to you? Well, let's say you analyze your results and find out that your most profitable customers are typically:

White, aged 45-50, have 2-3 children, are married, live on the northeast side of town, make between $75,000 to $100,000 a year, are active in the community, especially with charitable events, typically play a lot of golf and/or tennis, are conservative republicans, and often take 2-3 vacations a year.

That's some valuable information, I tell you. For starters, did you know you can rent a list in your area with those "selects" where select is just a fancy term for different attributes.

Yes, for a fee you could get a list of all the people in your city that are between 45-50, living in a certain zip code, making an annual income of $75,000 to $100,000 a year. And that's just a few of the "selects" you can specify. You can even go deeper if you wish.

These are the type of prospects you most definitely want to spend your money marketing to. While past results do not necessarily guarantee future behavior, they are about as good an indicator to go by as any. The point is, if that type of customer was profitable to you in the past, it stands to reason similar people who fit that description will also be extremely profitable for you today.

Then what do you do? The best thing is to create a direct mail campaign and send a letter to each name on the list you rented making them a special offer of some kind.

You want to write an advertisement that is personable, explains the benefits of your services, and makes a special "introductory offer" to get them into your place of business.

Even better is if, in those advertisements, you talk about things like golf and tennis, taking vacations, saying things that conservative republicans are known to agree with, and talk about charitable events.

This helps build rapport with those prospect. You just have to tie those things to your sales message and offer in some creative way.

And that's just one simple example of how to make the old "80/20" rule work in your favor.

Here's an even better example: Look into your customer records of your most profitable customers and ask yourself, "What services and goods can I offer them that they don't currently have, but would be complementary to purchases they've made in the past?"

If someone is a very profitable customer to you, it usually means that they like doing business with you, need a lot of what you have to offer, trust you, and often think of you as the "go-to" solution for problems related to your area of service and expertise.

So if you have a good recommendation that could help bring them value to their life, and is a perfect fit for something you've offered them in the past, you're likely to meet with success.

Here's how you can maximize your efforts. Start with your top 20 customers. What you want to do is write them a personal letter to each of them. Start with talking about how you were analyzing your past records and noticed that they have been a very good customer, and that you value their business. Then say you also noticed something that may be a benefit, and since they've been a good customer, you're going to give them a special deal next time they come into the store and purchase something for you. Give them specific examples, such as,

"I noticed you purchased XYZ from us. Well a new product we just got rights to complements XYZ perfectly, so if you come in within the next 2 weeks I can give you a special deal of 40% off the shelf price. This is just my way of saying thanks for being such a valuable customer."

Another strategy to consider is the referral strategy. Think about this: people typically hang around others who share their same values and beliefs. This is a perfect way to attract new customers who are likely to be just as profitable as your past "most profitable customers".

In this case, you'd send your best customers a letter, and let them know that you're making them a "valued customer special offer" if they recommend someone to your business, and you'll give their referrals a "preferred VIP discount" or "preferred VIP treatment", since they came from a highly valued source.

People love to refer when this is the case. It makes them look good in front of their friends, and a lot of people get value in that. It's also great for you, because word of mouth advertising is some of the best advertising there is. Also, if you can just get these referrals into the door and have them start a buying relationship with you, chances are they will continue to buy from you in the future. Thus you will get more than just a one-off purchase, you may get a customer for life with a high lifetime value.

The Referral Marketing Goldmine

The power of "Word of Mouth"

Referrals are the cheapest, yet the most effective marketing strategy in the world.

The idea is that you should be generating a large portion of your new customers by marketing to your existing customers.

There are several reasons why this is smart to do. First, quality attracts quality. Psychologists say that you are basically a combination of your five closest friends. In other words, people will refer people who are similar to them.

So if you have a big spender, then guess what? They'll probably refer other big spenders. Every good customer should be actively pursued for a referral because they'll usually generate other customers of equal character, quality and value.

Also, almost any marketing is usually met with skepticism. That's because you are often tooting your horn. But what if some one else was tooting your horn for you?

Know this – people are more likely to believe in you if someone else endorses your quality than if you yourself brag about your own qualities.

What you're really doing is leveraging off of someone else credibility. People who take the recommendations of their friends are now coming to you with a preconceived notion that you're already quality – before you even have to open your mouth.

Finally word of mouth marketing is target marketing. Basically, you're only going to be getting people who already are in the market for what you're offering. Mass marketing does not have this effect. If you run an ad on television, you're getting everybody who watches TV at that moment.

But with referral marketing, you're pretty much only getting people who are already great matches to your products or services. This means your closing rate will go up without having to learn one single bit of salesmanship. You're just getting people who are already more likely to say "yes" before they even enter into the store.

Okay, know my rule of thumb when it comes to referral marketing – every good customer should get three direct chances to refer someone else to you.

I have found in order to get the best results, you have to ask someone three times to make a referral on your behalf. If you do nothing else, you should do at least this.

However, to really make it effective, there are two more things you need to do: make it easy for them to refer, and make it worthwhile to refer. I'm going to show you how to do all of this and more, as I outline what I have found time and time again to be a profit pulling monster when it comes to referral systems.

The Referral System, Step by Step

First, get your metrics in order. How much money can you afford to spend on marketing for next month? Whatever it is, devote the largest portion of it to your referral marketing. So step one, find or establish your marketing budget.

Now, the specific plan I'm going to lay out to you is going to cost around $8 per person to perform. So if you have a budget of $800 for marketing, then you can reach roughly 100 people.

Start small and scale up – that's my advice. Don't spend too much upfront until you get back some reliable figures, and you can do some testing in between. Since this is a system, every dollar you spend will be tracked and traced back to determine the return on investment.

Here's how it works. Someone comes in and buys from you. Immediately the next day, you send them out a letter in the mail. You thank them, ask for referral, make it easy for them to refer, and then make it worth their while.

The most important part here is that it's in their best interest to refer others to you. For that to happen, first and foremost you must have provided quality and value. So I'm going to assume you're performing good service and living up to your end of the deal.

Second, gifts work wonders. My favorite kind of gifts are those that either cost me nothing or very little, but have a huge perception of value. Without a doubt, there is one gift I can consistently create for basically nothing, and it always does the necessary trick.

Coupon Books

It works like this – you go around to different business owners and tell them that you want to make sure your customers shop locally. As a thank you gift for your customers, you'd like to give them coupons or special offers from other local merchants, so you're providing your customers with value, and also keeping business local.

Then you simply ask them if they have any coupons or anything they'd like to contribute to your "customer gift book".

Almost every business owner you talk to will take you up on this. Why? Well, most businesses are not good at marketing, and to make up for it they always have a special going on, or are willing to do anything if it means getting a few more customers in the store.

Besides, you only need to get like 15 or 20 different coupons anyway to make a great gift book. You can get this all done in a few hours.

So now you have a great gift that you can give to anybody who sends a referral your way. How much did it cost you? Just the cost to print up the coupons and mail them. So you just made a gift of high perceived value (everybody loves coupons) that costs you about $1 to create and a few hours of sweat equity, thus, it's worth their while.

Now let's take a look at what the first referral letter should look like:

Dear Jill Customer,

The other day you made a purchase from our store, and we just wanted to say thank you from the bottom of our hearts for doing business with us. If there is anything you ever need in the future, please do not hesitate to call us up and ask. We'll see what we can do.

You may not know it, but the lifeline of our business comes from referrals. If you happen to know anyone else who could use our services, I'd be extremely happy to sit down and talk with them to see if we might be able to help them in any way.

And, if it so happens that the person you refer becomes our customer, then as a token of my appreciation I will send you my special "valued customer gift book", which has a total of over $250 off coupons for discounts from local businesses of all kinds.

I'll give the same gift to your friend as well.

It's really easy to refer someone to us. I've enclosed two of my business cards with your name written on the back of them. Just give them to anyone who you think could use our services. Just have them present the business card when they come in, so we know it was you that referred them.

Anyway, I just wanted to say thanks again for deciding to go with us.

Thanks,

Jim Business Owner

There is a lot of psychology that is going on in this first letter that I don't want you to miss.

First, it's personal and it's sincere. How many businesses have you bought something from in the last sixty days that sent you a personal thank you letter in the mail?

Hmmm... maybe 1 or 2 you might say?

So imagine what kind of impact that your letter has when it lands in your customer's mailbox. Big impact. It says you care. Do you know why most people leave a service provider?

A few die. Some move away. Others leave because of an unresolved complaint. A handful will be stolen away by a competitor. Now add all those up, and guess what?

It usually only comes to 32% of all total customers who leave you. So what about the other 68%?

They leave simply because you never have taken the time to recognize them as something more than a customer.

Pop quiz – If you had an unresolved complain, a direct competitor in your store trying to steal your customer, or the opportunity to let someone who purchased from you know you care... and you can only choose one option... which one should you choose?

You better choose the third option because roughly only 9% leave because of competition, and only 14% leave because of unresolved complaints.

If you do nothing else but keep in contact with your past customers and treat them as your friends and acknowledge them once in a while, you'll be putting the "golden handcuffs" on 2/3 of your customers, so you can keep selling to them again and again. Think of their lifetime value.

If you get nothing else out of the referral letter, you will get that personal communication that will separate you from 90% of all businesses, and almost every single one of your competitors.

The second thing that letter does is conveys your expectations. You expect all of your customers to refer. Most people don't refer simply because they don't know you want them to refer. In fact, I've had customers come up and tell my clients -- "Heck, I thought you already had enough customers, or I didn't know you could take on more"

You should seen that business owner slap his forehead.

Once people know that you want them to refer, you automatically increase the chances they will refer, even if it isn't immediate. Again, I've had people hold on to business cards for two or three years before they gave one to someone else.

Also, notice the casual tone of the letter. People prefer doing business with friends, and not faceless corporations.

Finally, it shows you care. The above letter basically says, "Hey, I know you're busy and I know you got to look out for your own self interests. That's why I've gone the extra mile to make it in your own self interest to refer to me."

Ideally, you don't want to take the above letter word for word. You want to fill in "our services" with your actual services and so forth. But I give you permission to take most of the above verbatim and use it.

But don't stop there. After the first letter is sent out, wait 10-15 days. If you haven't gotten a referral from them yet, then send them letter two

www.cyconsocialmedia.com

Dear Jill Customer,

A few weeks ago I sent you a letter thanking you for your purchase. I hope you got everything you wanted out of it and more. Remember – if you ever need help with anything, I'm only a phone call away.

We've also sent out several "customer gift books" in the last few weeks to our valued customers who referred one of their friends to us.

I know things can get busy, and sometimes stuff can get misplaced in the shuffle. To make sure you don't miss out on your own special customer gift book, I've sent you two more business cards with your name on the back – just in case you misplaced the last two I sent you.

Just give those to a friend in need, if you think we can help them, and we'll mail you your "customer gift book" pronto!

Once again, I just wanted to say thanks for being our customer, and we hope that we can continue to provide you with more service in the years to come.

Thanks,

Jim Business Owner

Here's what I know about marketing – one-shot advertising is not very effective. It's not that people don't want to act on your offers. A lot of them do. What happens is that the day to day details take over, and what they intend on doing ends up getting pushed to the back of their mind.

What this letter does is thank them again, puts you in front of them again, and basically let's them off the hook – hey, it wasn't their fault. You know they're busy people.

Also, it gives you another excuse to send them two more business cards. It also offers some social proof "hey, everybody else is referring".

Every time we track these campaigns, we usually find something like this – we get 3% to refer off the first letter. We get 4% to refer off the second letter, and we get 2% to refer off the third. In any case, all mailings are profitable.

Now think – if we just stopped after the first time, we'd get a measly 3% response. But instead we got a 9% response. In most scenarios, it almost always plays out that the second letter will work the best. Who knows why – it just does.

Now those who didn't respond to letter number one, and don't respond to letter number two, will get, after 10-15 more days, the third and last letter:

Dear Jill Customer,

Hope everything is going great for you. The reason I'm writing to you today is because I had a few "customer gift books" left over and didn't want them to go to waste.

I had one specifically set aside for you, so I have enclosed it with this letter. It is just our way of saying thanks for being a great customer.

Also, just in case you lost the last cards in the laundry or something, I've put in two more business cards with your name on the back.

Just pass them on to a friend if they're ever in need of any of the services that we offer…We'll make sure to treat them right.

Thanks!

Jim Business Man

Now, I don't want you to confuse the technique with the strategy. This works because:

- It puts you in front of them 3 times.
- It conveys the expectation that they will refer.

- It is personal and friendly.

- It is easy to do.

- It is in their own best interest.

You don't have to do the coupon gift book. Sometimes I'll just purchase tickets for a special upcoming local event, or event complimentary dinners at a good local restaurant.

Lastly, a few more pointers – make your letters look like personal letters. This means, when you design the layout, don't put some fancy "brochure" feel into it. Just picture how you'd design the letter if you were going to sit down and write a good friend a personal note.

Also, when you get this system in place, you'll get some numbers. You might find for every 5 customers you do this for, you get 1 referral in the next 30 days. Okay, do that math – let's say your average sale netted you $600 in profits.

And let's say when you deduct all marketing expenses for creating and mailing those letters, it cost you $100. That's a 6 to 1 return on investment. Try getting that with other types of advertising.

This type of marketing also allows you to test different approaches. What would happen if you altered the gift? You can literally test every element you want, and know what is working and what isn't working. This means you can figure out the exact combination of steps for getting the greatest return on your investment.

How to Tear Down Customer Resistance

How many of the people who walk into your business, or who take an interest in your products and services, end up going ahead with a purchase? In sales, this is called a closing rate.

To manage something, you first have to measure it. That way you know where it's at present, so you know what you need to do to improve it.

So here's a simple question you need to have an answer to – if 10 prospects are interested in doing business with you, on average how many out of those 10 actually end up doing business with you?

The percentage itself isn't important. In stores with a lot of traffic, you can do 1 out of 10 and be fine. I have a website where I do 1 out of 100, and it's good enough for me to make a great return on investment, because it takes hardly any time or effort on my part. In some businesses, you need 5 out of 10 just to have a chance at making any profit at all.

What is important is knowing how to improve your percentages to a more "acceptable" range. So if you get 5 out of 10, do the math and see how much more you'd make if you got 6 out of 10. Since they're already coming in the door, most of the work is done. You're just looking for those "little things" to get more people converted into paying customers.

There are a lot of different ways to improve your closing rate, and some are more complicated than others. I always look for the "80/20" factor in any given task. In other words I'm looking for that one or two key things that will make most of the difference between someone purchasing from you or not. Here's some insight to help you discover that "vital one thing" that gives you a majority of your results.

Do you know what three things are required before a prospect becomes a customer? Knowing this will give you the answer you need. Here are the three things that are needed:

First, they have to want what you offer.

Second, they have to have money to purchase it.

Third, they have to believe that you'll actually come through on your end of the deal.

The more inclined they are to already want what you have, the easier it is to sell to them. The more money they have set aside for making consumer purchases, the easier it to the sell to them. The more they believe that you actually will deliver on your offer, the easier it is to sell to them.

I have before me a phone book with yellow page ads. I'm going to flip through it and quote some phrases. Here's are just a few and the thoughts :

- "Dependable & Quality Service"

And here's what your typical savvy potential customer is thinking:

"Oh yeah!? Says who?"

- "Value, Service & Convenience"

This description is meaningless, and everybody knows it. They're thinking :

"Prove It!"

- "Friendly service"

Once again, consumers have heard this all before, and they are thinking:

"Yeah, right!

In other words, these are hollow phrases of puffery that everybody uses. It's so easy to say those things, and so saying those things mean very little or nothing. I've actually called a business whose yellow page ad said "friendly service" only to be treated rudely by the receptionist who answered the phone. Guess someone forgot to tell her.

So how do you go beyond mere puffery and actually prove your case that you're friendlier, more valuable, offer better service and are more dependable than every other option they have available at their fingertips?

Well, I'll share with you one simple way to do this that will drastically differentiate you from every competitor, both direct and indirect. As a bonus, it's also very simple to do, it is extremely cost effective and when compiled, can be used in a variety of different outlets and mediums. What I'm talking about is customer testimonials.

Selling Power of Testimonials

If you want to increase your closing rates without resorting to any fancy tricks or learning a bunch of new skills, just start being an avid collector of testimonials.

I don't care what anyone else says, they still work.

Consider this – what if I told you I was the greatest marketing consultant of all time? Would you really believe me? What if your friend called you up and told you I was the greatest marketing consultant? Then you might believe it.

But what if your lawyer, your doctor, your mother, your children school principal, the head of your trade association and the guy you buy bell peppers from at the local farmer's market told you I was the greatest marketing consultant of all time? I have no doubt you'd believe it.

I bet you'd be really interested in sitting down and having a talk with me, wouldn't you? You'd probably think a great deal more of me than if I just call you up and brag about my skills.

This is such a simple principle, it makes me wonder – why don't all businesses use testimonials? I don't know why. I think it should be a requirement of doing business personally. That is because, when it comes to raising your closing rates, it makes all the difference.

Now let me show you when, where and how to get these killer testimonials that will increase the believability of your offers.

How to Become an Avid Testimonial Collector

If you go looking for opportunities to get testimonials, you'll find it's easy to begin collecting them.

The best opportunity is when your customer is "in heat". What I mean by this is that you've just done something that has "wowed" them. They might come in to pay their bill and say "I can't believe what a wonderful service you did. It's better than the last five people I've gone to!"

There is your chance. You say: "Thanks! Would it be okay if I shared your story with others who might be interested in our services as well? It really helps us better serve our clients."

Or, you can say: "Thanks. Would it be okay if I wrote down what you just said and shared it with others? It would mean a lot to me." Then just write down really quickly what was said, and have them approve it.

Or you can simply say: "Thanks. Did you know that one of the best ways we get good clients just like you is sharing the success stories of our past clients? Would it be okay if we quoted you in some of our marketing and sales communications?"

Don't make it harder than it has to be. The main process is – get them when they're in a good mood. Ask if you can have their permission to quote them and share their story. Then get their testimonial. That's it.

Also, it's smart if you ask them if you can share their name with others as well, just to be on the safe side.

If you do nothing else, just collect testimonials from customers who are in heat and have just expressed how appreciative they are of you and your services.

Another good time is when you "save the day". Did you do something for a customer that was out of the ordinary? Maybe you made a house call at 8:30 at night to fix an emergency, free of charge. Or perhaps they wanted something that was supposedly discontinued, but you went the extra mile and tracked down what they were looking for.

Anytime you save the day, just ask them for a testimonial. In fact, I intentionally look for opportunities to save the day, because it serves in my self interest. If I go the extra mile, then I know they'll give me one heck of a testimonial.

Once you get good at the first two, consider sending out a customer survey once in a while. Have them answer a few key questions. Then, retype those answers up in a letter form, and ask them to sign off on it as a testimonial that you can share with others.

There are more aggressive ways to get testimonials, and I would encourage you to be aggressive about getting them, especially after you've gotten the knack for getting the low hanging fruit. Once you get used to asking your "in heat customers" and those who you've "saved the day for", experiment with actively seeking out testimonials to further prove your case.

How to Use Testimonials for Maximum Effect

I'm going to give you some examples that you can literally knock off and use in your own business, and also that you can use to brainstorm your own ideas from.

Let's return to the yellow book example. Instead of the typical puffery, your ad might include something that says:

"Look, any business can say that they care about their customers and that they are dependable and have high quality service. Instead of us touting our own horn, maybe you'd rather hear it from some of our customers themselves. Just call our "satisfied customer hot line" to hear a pre-recorded message of what our customers think about our services."

You know how much a voice mail account costs? About $4 a month. For $4 a month, you can have a recording of your best customers. How do you get these recordings?

Perhaps you have your sales reps call your customers a few days after the sale. Explain to the customer that for quality issues, would it be okay if you recorded the call? This can be done inexpensively with a digital phone recorder that costs less than $50, or through an online service for about $10 a month.

Then, ask them what their thoughts were on the service or for the product. At the end, ask them if it would be okay if you shared their thoughts with others who might be interested in your products or services.

That's just one way to get your testimonials recorded. There are others.

Now you have a tool – you have people talking about how good you are. You can put this prerecorded message into all of your marketing communications. Your believability goes through the roof.

Here's something else you might want to consider – gathering up a "testimonial book".

Do you know any salesperson who has a testimonial book? Hmm... Wouldn't that distinguish you from every other competitor out there? I think it would and in a good way.

Let's say you really went the extra mile and totally knock it out of the park for a customer. They were so happy they called you up and thanked you personally, and said they were so impressed with you and that you went above and beyond the call of duty.

Well how about this – you ask them if it would be okay to feature them as "case study" in your next advertisement. Then you could write an advertisement that looks like an article, where you simply tell the story of what you did for this customer. This type of advertisement is about a million times more effective than "BUY MY PRODUCT!" advertisements you currently see everywhere.

At the very least, you should include some testimonials in your advertising, just to enhance your ordinary claims.

One person I knew went as far as recording on video his customer testimonials. Then, when someone didn't purchase the first time they came into his store, five days later they'd get the video in the mail that contained all these wonderful customer testimonials.

Needless to say, a lot of people came back and ended up purchasing who otherwise would not have.

Anatomy of a Good Testimonial

Now, some people have tried testimonials and have told me that they don't work. Well, it reminds me of my Dad telling me five years ago that his DVD player didn't work. I asked him -- "Did you plug it in?"

Oops!

Testimonials are like anything else – if you do them poorly then they probably won't work. In order to do them right, you must know what a good testimonial looks like.

Here's a bad testimonial:

"You did a good job!"

Here's a killer testimonial:

"You responded to our call and were at our house in 7 minutes. The last guys took 2 hours. Not only that, you helped us save 13% off the cost. Thanks a bunch!" -- Jim, Fire Fighter, Sacramento, CA.

The difference is obvious. Bad testimonials are bland and really don't say anything. Good testimonials are specific, and give you hard facts. I love it when someone says to me: "I read your book on Thursday, and by Saturday morning I did one thing I learned on page 8 that resulted in me making $15,867.13 in profit by the following Tuesday. You're a genius!".

That's a far better testimonial than "your ideas helped me make more money".

Not only is specificity needed, but it's good to have a name, location and occupation. Otherwise people will think that maybe you're just making up the testimonials yourself, even though that is illegal. Which is why audio and video testimonials are best.

Also, there are other things that can influence your testimonials. What's better – five testimonials featured in your ads from white males aged 43 and over, or a mix of ages, races and both males and females?

Well, it depends. If your product targets white males that are 43 years old, then it's a good idea. If it targets a wide variety of audiences, then you want testimonials from a wide variety of people.

Lastly, as humans we're hardwired by nature to trust authority. That's why testimonials from scientists, doctors, nurses, fire fighters, and other esteemed positions tend to have more pull than regular testimonials from regular people. Just think how much more credible a testimonial is from a rocket scientist than a "sanitary engineer".

So set a plan – come up with different ways you're going to capture and use testimonials, and make sure everybody in your business starts to become a testimonial collector. It's one of the easiest ways to increase your sales closing percentage and profits.

Right Way to Place Yellow Page Ads

Have you noticed that 95% of Yellow Page ads look the same or look alike? There's a problem with going with the "norm" -- you get normal results.

With your business and livelihood on the line, I hope you're not content with average results, especially when extraordinary results are so easy to get with Yellow Pages. You only need to do a few simple things.

The first thing you have to understand is what people are looking for when they open up the yellow pages. Some people are looking for specific contact information. They already have a service provider in mind. It's hard to get those people.

But the good news is when most people open up the Yellow Pages, they are looking for information to help them find the best business to contact that will give them the solution they desire and need.

And here's what most consumers want: They want a good deal, they want to go with someone who is able to understand their needs and lead them to the best solution, and they want to deal with as little headaches, delays and customer service problems as possible.

Now, flip open your yellow pages and see if any of the ads address those points, and you'll find hardly any do so adequately and effectively.

Good. That will make it much easier for you.

I'm going to show you how to create a simple yellow page ad that will make people believe that if they contact you or go into your store that they are going to get the best solution for their dollars, and it's going to be easy and convenient to deal with you, and that you're the best choice for all of their options.

If you can pull that off, you're going to get the lion's share of Yellow Page customers in your industry.

Most Important Part of Your Ad

The world's best ad is no better than the world's worst ad if no one sees it. So the first job your Yellow Page ad must do is get the attention of the people who are best matched to take advantage of the services and products that you offer.

The easiest way to do that is with a good attention-getting headline.

To understand what a good headline looks like, first let's look at some bad headlines. I went through my own local Yellow Pages, and found these headlines:

"The Blind Factory"

"Cyclists Serving Cyclists"

"Wet Basement or Crawl Space"

"Quality Construction"

"Professional Muffler, Inc"

"Old Fashioned Values, Including Our Own People Doing the Work"

These are all terrible headlines. First, almost all of them talk about the service provider, and not the person who is looking at the ad. Talk about selfish and self-centered.

Second, none of them promise any benefit to the person, none of them get the person reading excited, and most are nothing more than the name of the company.

Your headline is the most important part of your yellow page ad so you need to do much better than that. Ideally, you want a headline that promises a benefit to the reader, and is written to grab the attention of a certain large segment of the population who is best matched for the goods and services you provide.

Let's look at the first one -- "The Blind Factory". How could this one be improved? Here is a good headline that I have found that gets great results. "The 6 Mistakes Most People Make When They Purchase Blinds For Their Home."

Or... "Warning: Don't Buy Any Blinds Until You Read This." Or Even "How to Get the Best Blinds For Your Home in 48 Hours Or Less, Guaranteed!"

Notice the difference with these headlines? First, they focus on the consumer. Second, they promise a huge benefit. Third, they call out a certain portion of the general population – in this case, people who are looking to purchase blinds, who want to get a good deal, want ease of service, or want to make sure they don't commit a mistake when buying blinds.

Once you have a good headline, the ad practically writes itself. For example, let's return to the headline: "The 6 Mistakes People Make When They Purchase Blinds for Their Home". You would then come up with 6 mistakes that you find people tend to make if they don't have an expert to help them select their product. And then, after you introduce each mistake, explain how that mistake can be avoided if they come into your store.

Remember, people who open up the Yellow Page ads are generally looking for information to help them make the best decision on who to buy from. So typically the person who provides the most information wins and it helps if that information is all beneficial to the reader.

But if you look at the typical Yellow Page ad, it has 50 words or less, and is usually filled with puffery. For example, I always see "The customer comes first". And I always say – prove it.

Which leads us to the second biggest point about writing effective Yellow Pages ads: making powerful, unique claims to demonstrate that you're better than any other solution that's available in the Yellow Pages.

So how can you make a unique claim that demonstrates that "the customer comes first". Here's a technique that's been used to great effect. The first thing you do is contact some of your past satisfied customers. Then, you ask them to write a quick one paragraph testimonial about what they liked most about dealing with you. It's easy to do this with the right strategy.

Then, you put all those testimonials on a website. Now, in your ad you can say, "You can even read what 117 satisfied customers had to say about our great products at..." and then put the website address in there.

Now, most people looking at the ad won't go to page and read it. But it will have the effect of demonstrating to them that not only does the customer come first, but you have 117 of your own customers who say that you do put them first. You'll be the only ad in your category that can claim that, so in people's minds you'll be the preferred source if customer service is their main priority.

At any rate, your ad should contain at least one dramatic example of proof to validate your claims. It's best if you have specific numbers or facts to verify it, testimonials to show and other powerful ways to demonstrate that you offer great service and goods.

For example, you can do much better than merely stating something like "In business since 1972!" My first reaction when I see this statement is "So what?"

The fact is, I know a lot of bad companies that have stayed in business for decades. Instead, you can say "We've successfully helped over 10,678 clients in Houston find the right blinds for their homes."

So first come up with a powerful headline. Then, expand on that headline in your ad, and also throw in at least one dramatic example of proof to validate your claims.

Now you only have to do one final thing.

Have an Offer And a "Call To Action"

Every single ad you write should have an offer and a call-to-action to accept that offer. A call to action means that you tell them exactly what they should do after reading the ad.

Let me start with the best call to action, although it's also the most complicated one to set up.

What you ideally want is a continuing relationship with people who are interested in doing business with you, so if they are hesitant initially, further communication can get them in the door.

The best way to do that is to offer something free to the user if they contact you. Here's a simple way to do that. Let's go back to the Blinds example.

The first thing you'd want to do is sit down and write a little 6-8 page report on "How to Pick The Most Beautiful Blinds For Your Home On A Shoe-string Budget" or something along those lines.

Then just give them the best tips for getting the most value from their purchase.

What you're going to want to do next is take that report and export it as PDF (you can do this for free with OpenOffice, which you can download from the Internet).

Then, you're going to want to set up an "autoresponder" account at aweber.com or getresponse.com or some other service. This allows you to have people sign up for an email list, so you can send them emails in the future.

Then, if they sign up for your list, they will automatically get delivered your free digital report on "How to Pick The Most Beautiful Blinds For Your Home On A Shoe-string Budget." Not only that, you can use your autoresponder to send a few follow up messages automatically at certain intervals to anyone who signs up and promote your current events.

Then in your Yellow Page ad you say, "If you'd like to get our free report on "How to Pick The Most Beautiful Blinds For Your Home On A Shoe-string Budget", then just go to www.your websiteaddress.com". This drives them to a page that explains that in order to get the report they just have to enter in their name and email into the form.

Of course, in the report you're going to want to put your contact information so if they read it they can easily contact you and become your customer.

This is by far the best strategy but also the most complex. A simple strategy is to make a "Yellow Page ad only" offer. In this case you say, "If you call us today to schedule an appointment, and mention that you are calling because of the Yellow Page ad, we'll give a 10% off Yellow Page 'special deal".

In any case, you're enticing them to respond to your ad.

If you do all of the things in this book, then you're going to have an ad that is dramatically different than everyone else's which will allow you to get dramatically different and better results.

5 Proven Internet Strategies to Explode Your Local Sales

#1 Video Marketing

Would you believe that there are over 26 billion videos viewed per month in the United States alone? What's more, YouTube is the #4 search engine on the Internet, which means that right now somebody is likely searching for your services online in the form of a video.

Imagine if you had the budget to run infomercials 24 hours a day, 7 days a week, you'd dominate your market. That's the power of video marketing. Let me show you how this is possible on a shoestring even in a terrible economy, and be able to engender more trust and respect with your customers than ever before.

#2 *Lead-Capture and Follow-up Campaigns*

Did you know that even great webpage will only convert 5% of it's visitors to a purchase. It's absolutely true, and this means that 19 out of 20 visitors to your website are destined to surf away into the ether, and likely find your competitor's website instead.

However the average page that offers consumers free information in exchange for their contact info gets 35-40% conversion.

Imagine being able to instantly increase your return on leads 7-fold, and do it with push button automation. This is possible, and I can show you how.

3 Local Search Visibility

Did you know that 30% of all searches online include a city or local term like "Houston Plumbing Contractors"?

This means that every search for every term will have local companies that have figured out how to get listed in all of the local directories.

It goes without saying that your customers can't hire you if they can't find you online. I can make sure that your local business is found on Google for all of the keywords that you need to rank for so that your neighbors can find you online.

#4 *Social Media Marketing*

With over 800,000,000 members and growing fast, Facebook is a giant that cannot be ignored. Social networks have changed the way people research and make buying decisions.

When leveraged in your favor you'll have the opportunity to build more trust, respect, and credibility than ever before.

Imagine being able to have feedback on how to improve your business, and sell more on a daily basis. Imagine being able to turn every customer into a potential raving fan who will advertise for you. I can make it happen, and you can secure my services exclusively in your local market.

#5 Blog Marketing

Did you know that 77% of all Internet users follow one or more blogs? If you're not capitalizing on the growing community, you're missing out on huge business opportunity.

Bloggers are passionate about sharing, and if you have one as a client and can turn them into a raving fan, they can propel your business to all new heights.

Let me help you create and manage your article or video blog, all with push-button simplicity so you can leverage this influence-engine giant for your benefit. And increase your bottom line year after year.

About the Author

Author, consultant, and online marketing pro, Duke Morris is an expert at helping small businesses gain dominant position in their local marketplace.

Duke specializes in helping entrepreneurs and small businesses gain competitive advantage in their both online and offline market position. He makes sure that these businesses are able to be "found" on the Internet, ensures that they never run out of leads, and helps them to transform these potential clients into lifetime customers and raving fans.

If you are serious about improving your own business' bottom line, and would like to schedule a free consultation to see how Duke can set a comprehensive online marketing campaign for your company, you can contact him by leaving your name, telephone and email address at www.cyconsocialmedia.com, or by leaving a voicemail at 281.891.3111.

Good selling!

Other books published by Duke Morris:

Small Business.com

Social Media Marketing

Text Message Marketing

YouTube Marketing

Don't Make $100K Mistake when searching for a job

All books available at Amazon and other fine bookstores.

Small Business Resources

http://www.sba.gov

Small business is America's most powerful engine of opportunity and economic growth. That's where SBA comes in. SBA offers a variety of programs and support services to help you navigate the issues you face with your initial applications, and resources to help after you open for business.

http://www.score.org

SCORE is a nonprofit association dedicated to helping small businesses get off the ground, grow and achieve their goals through education and mentorship. They have been doing this for nearly fifty years.

Because their work is supported by the U.S. Small Business Administration (SBA), and thanks to huge network of 13,000+ volunteers, they are able to deliver these services at no charge or at very low cost.

http://www.irs.gov/Businesses/Small-Businesses-&-Self-Employed/Other-Government-Resources

Like it or not you will have to deal with IRS. Why not explore free advice and explanation of your duties as a small business owner.

They offer free video, webinars and audio presentations for small businesses, individuals & tax pros. Workshops and webinars on a variety of topics for small businesses.

You can choose from a variety of products, including the Tax Calendar desktop tool, to help you learn about business taxes on your own time, and at your own pace.

http://www.osha.gov/dcsp/smallbusiness/index.html

(http://www.dol.gov/oasam/programs/osdbu/sbrefa/#.Ukgcftbifdq)

OSHA resources and information are designed specifically for small business employers, including safety and health tools and publications, easy-to-follow guides for specific OSHA standards, and descriptions of benefits that small businesses receive from OSHA.

OSHA's Free On-site Consultation Program provides on-site assistance to small business employers in protecting their workers from potential occupational hazards.

http://www.inc.com

Popular business magazine with fresh and useful information, comments and tools.

http://www.nfib.com

National Federation of Independent Business provides huge variety of business resources. How-to tips and info you need to run your small business. From finance help to sales advice to staffing.

http://www.entrepreneur.com

Tons of editorial coverage and contributions on variety of topics of interest to small businesses, like: Startups, Run & Grow, Money, Marketing, Technology, Franchises etc.

www.cyconsocialmedia.com

www.cyconsocialmedia.com

www.ingramcontent.com/pod-product-compliance
Lightning Source LLC
Chambersburg PA
CBHW061516180526
45171CB00001B/211